FINDING THE RIGHT ILLUSTRATOR

① When the author and the editor are satisfied that the s
is the best the author can make it, then the editor ha
find the right illustrator.

Finding the right illustrator

② This is not always as easy as it sounds because the i
must like the author's story - it's no use trying to
something you don't like because it shows in the work
The illustrator must have an understanding of the au
words, he must be able to bring those words to life,
~~as being capable of adding~~ all those little extras t
~~author meant to put in~~ belong with the story, even thoug
~~~~ not have mentioned them.

③ For Nan Hunt's story <u>Whistle Up The Chimney</u>, I need
illustrator who liked the story, who could draw st
as well as people, and who had an imagination and a
visualise ?
fun to appreciate and ~~bring life~~ to Nan's marvello
I found the ideal illustrator in Craig Smith.

④ If you look at a copy of <u>Whistle Up The Chimney</u>,
a lovely, ginger tom cat on almost every page, h
when you read the text you will find that Nan Hu
mentions a cat. Craig added him and gave him s
personality that Nan had to sit down and write
for him - and that was how the second book, An
was born, ~~and Tom Bola became a cat we all love~~
which tells how Tom Bola escapes on a runaway trai

Finding the right illustrator can take a long
years, so the author has to learn to be very !
when the editor has found an illustrator, it
illustrator months to think through his ideas
on paper. Quite often, even though he loves
illustrator may not be able to put the right
Then the editor has to say "No" and start lo
else.

It is essential that the illustrator plan
<u>before</u> he starts to paint. If he doesn't,
to run out of pages halfway through, or finish too soon
and have pages to spare.

When planning each opening the illustrator has a lot to
think about. He must be certain that he is illustrating
the words he wants on that page. He must also be aware
of the important parts of the story and not have half the
text on one page and half on the next, and so upset the ~~climax.~~
flow of the story.

There is no need for the illustrator to put the text on one
page and his artwork on the other, although it sometimes
works best this way. The whole book must be thought through
and planned, not only by the illustrator but also by the
editor and the designer - it is a team effort.

Why 32 pages?
Most books are made of sections of 8, 16 or 32 pages. This is because of the way the paper is folded. Take an ordinary sheet of paper. Try folding it four times as shown. How many pages do you have now?

any anecdotes about illustrators missing important cues in the text? e.g. hair colouring, age of children in story, details of location, getting the mood right? Can't think of one at the moment.

a gull - needs to be done by artist

pix

suggest a box with text similiar to this

You do come back to this later (pp 27 ff) but some explanation is needed here

etc to end up with a sheet folded into 32 pages.

Books are printed on big sheets, usually 16 pages at a time, then folded & the edges trimmed.

MAKING A PICTURE BOOK

 Design by
Black Cockatoo

COLLINS PUBLISHERS AUSTRALIA
First published in 1987 by
METHUEN AUSTRALIA
This edition published in 1989
by William Collins Pty Ltd
55 Clarence Street Sydney NSW 2000

Typeset by Midland Typesetters
in Paladium 12pt and Souvenir Light 12pt
Illustrations are done in pen and wash

Produced by Mandarin Offset, Hong Kong

National Library of Australia
Cataloguing-in-Publication data:

Ingram, Anne Bower.
    Making a picture book.

    Includes index.
    ISBN 0 7322 7335 8

    1. Publishers and publishing - Juvenile literature.
    2. Picture-books for children - Juvenile literature.
    3. Children's literature - Technique - Juvenile
    literature. I. Graham, Bob, 1942-   . II. Title.

070.5

MAKING A PICTURE BOOK

Anne Bower Ingram

Illustrated by Bob Graham

Collins
Publishers
Australia

For Peg, a true friend

Contents

How many people make a book?

If you want to make a book you need a team. A team that works together like a cricket team or a netball team. Everyone has a particular job to do.

There is an author, who writes down her story which she sends to . . .

the editor, who works for a publishing house. The editor then looks for . . .

So is the production manager, who advises about the shape of the book and its cost.

Then there is the typesetter, who sets the story in type.

And the printer, who prints the book.

an illustrator, who reads the author's story and starts to sketch his ideas . . .

he also works closely with the editor who makes sure that the illustrator doesn't forget about the author's story.

The designer is there to help the illustrator with his ideas.

Then all the books are stored in the warehouse, before they are sent to . . .

the bookshops where the bookseller sells them to . . .

your parents,
your teachers,
your librarians,   and to you.

The publishing house

The publishing house provides the money to make and sell a book. It also gives the help that an author and an illustrator need to turn their ideas into a finished book that can be sold by the bookseller.

There are many departments inside a publishing house, each with its own particular tasks.

It's really like a big family, each member of which has a specific job to do, all working together under the same roof, to make the best book possible.

A publishing house looks like this:

9

What does an editor do?

The editor is the person who decides whether the publishing house will take the story that an author has sent in and turn it into a book.

If the editor likes the story she then has to work with the author correcting any mistakes, and helping the author to make it the best story she can write. Sometimes authors do strange things, like saying that one of their characters has blue eyes, then later on in the story saying they have brown eyes.

To do all this the editor and the author have to work closely together — they must be good friends and trust each other.

Every story is very special and very precious to its author. It's really like a baby to them because it has been created out of their imagination and it has taken a lot of time and effort to write. The editor must understand all this, especially when she suggests that the author re-write parts of the story.

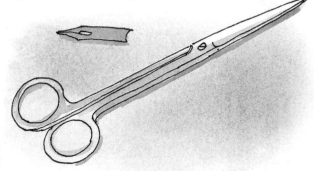

The editor checks spelling, punctuation and grammar.

Sometimes the editor has to suggest some changes.

They are both enthusiastic about the story.

The editor and the author meet, if they can, to discuss the story.

She sees that the story is consistent and makes sense.

The author and the editor need to trust each other.

Sometimes the author needs to rewrite part of the story after discussing it with the editor.

If often takes many drafts to get the story right.

Once the editor and author are both certain that the story is right, then the editor has to find an illustrator and work with him—encouraging, advising and helping when needed.

At this time the editor and the designer are also working together, because the illustrator needs to talk with the designer to solve some of the technical details. Things like the size and shape of the typeface that will be used, the shape of the book, and the weight of the paper.

The editor and designer then work with the production department, giving them all the details about the book so that they can work out what the costs will be and arrange for the story to be typeset, for the printing to be done, and for the finished books to be shipped to the warehouse.

Finally, the editor talks to the salespeople. She tells them all about the book, its author and its illustrator. The editor tries to make the salespeople very enthusiastic about this book so that they will sell it to the bookseller who will then sell it to you.

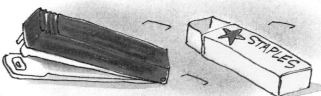

11

Where do the stories come from?

Where do the stories come from that the publishing house turns into books? The finding of these stories, or manuscripts, is one of the jobs of the editor, and there are several ways she goes about it.

- An editor always has a 'stable' of authors who will mostly write and work for her. This means there are always new stories available.
- Sometimes the editor will approach a well-known author and ask (or commission) her to write a particular story.
- At other times the editor will have an idea and then she finds an author to write that story.
- Then there are the stories that are sent into the publishing house by people who want to be writers.

All over the world there are authors, sitting in front of typewriters or word processors, writing stories. When they have finished they post their story to a publishing house.

Hundreds of these unsolicited stories arrive every year. So that they don't become lost, each story is carefully looked after. It is recorded in a logbook, then passed to an editor who reads it carefully and decides what is to be done to it.

If it is no good it is returned to the author with a rejection letter. However, sometimes a story may be very good but the editor has just published something similar. Then she returns the story to the author and suggests that she send it to another publishing house.

There are also times when an editor receives a story that she can't publish because it doesn't fit in with the type of books her publishing house sells. Then she suggests that author goes to someone who publishes that style of book.

When the editor finds a story that is just right for her list, she is very excited and immediately contacts the author and they begin working together.

Sometimes an author will have to send her story to several publishers before it is accepted. This happened to Mem Fox's story for *Possum Magic*. It was sent to ten publishers before it was finally accepted.

Also, Mem re-wrote that story twenty-five times before both she and her editor were happy with it. In Mem's original story the main character was a mouse, not a possum. It was her editor's suggestion to make the change.

Possum Magic shows us that if a story or an idea is a good one, then it will eventually be found and published, even if it takes many years and many re-writes.

Possum Magic began life as *Hush the Invisible Mouse*. The author, Mem Fox, sent her story to ten different publishers. Mem's editor suggested changing Hush to an Australian animal because there were already hundreds of mouse stories. Mem chose a possum because at the time she had lots of possums living in her roof.

Here is one of Julie Vivas's illustrations for Hush when he was a mouse and (at left) the illustration that finally appeared in the book.

Possum Magic

Written by Mem Fox   Illustrated by Julie Vivas

Ideas: where do you find them?

Nan Hunt's story idea came with a load of old firewood.

A bogey louvre

WHISTLE UP THE CHIMNEY

by Nan Hunt
Illustrations by Craig Smith

Every story comes from an idea, therefore every author needs to have lots of good ideas if they want to write interesting and exciting stories.

Nan Hunt is an author with hundreds of story ideas, as well as a vivid imagination. Many of her ideas have the strangest beginnings. Take, for example, *Whistle up the Chimney*. This story came about because Nan lives in a country town with long, cold winters.

Early one March, Nan ordered a load of firewood ready for the winter. When it arrived she found it was full of old railway sleepers and even parts from old railway carriages. The men who delivered it said the local railway yard was having a clean-up.

Nan stood watching the men throwing the load into the woodheap. Suddenly she saw something very special — half a door from a bogey louvre — and her imagination began running wild. 'My fire won't go crickle-crackle this winter,' Nan thought, 'it will go biddlydum-biddlydee.'

A bogey louvre was a special railway truck that was used before refrigerated trains were invented. It was ideal for sending fruit to market in because it kept the sun off the fruit while allowing the air to circulate.

Nan began sawing up her load of wood into fireplace lengths, but her mind was not on the job. Her ideas were whizzing around at a faster rate than the chainsaw she was using.

Finally Nan gave in and went to her study and began to write:

GHOST TRAINS   28/3/79

Mrs Millie Mack lived by herself in a little white house in a great big garden.

As she wrote, some questions kept coming into Nan's mind and she had to find the answers to them all . . .

- What would you do if you heard a train whistle in your chimney?
- How would a train get into your chimney?
- How do you make it appear?
- How do you write about the impossible?

Nan found the answers to all these questions as she wrote.

14

WHISTLE UP THE CHIMNEY
by Nan Hunt
Illustrations by Craig Smith

The revised draft of Nan Hunt's story (at right) involved a lot of changes, including the title.

~~GHOST TRAINS~~   28/3/79

HALF A DOOR FROM A BOGEY LOUVRE

Mrs Millie Mack lived by herself in a little white house in a ~~great~~ big garden

Her husband was dead and her children grown up and married.

Sometimes ~~the~~ children came *for a visit* and brought the grandchildren to see her.

In ~~the~~ spring Mrs Millie *Mack* planted ~~her~~ vegetables ~~garden~~ and *talked* ~~went round her~~ garden ~~flowers~~ /every day ~~to see how lovely the~~ *to the* ~~xxxxxxx blossoms~~ *flowers* ~~were~~.

In ~~the~~ summer she weeded and watered, picked ~~the~~ *flowers &* vegetables,

~~cut off the dead flower heads,~~ and made delicious raspberry jam.

In ~~the~~ autumn she preserved ~~the~~ fruit *until her/shelves were full pantry* and made jellies and jams, pickles and chutneys, ~~and~~ relishes and sauces.

She always had a jar to give away to friends or to put on ~~the~~ stall ~~for~~ *at* a fete.

Who Sank the Boat?
Pamela Allen

Jonah and the Manly Ferry
PETER GOULDTHORPE

Sometimes illustrators will write their own story. Instead of waiting for an editor to send them someone else's story they come up with their own ideas.

Pamela Allen is an illustrator who always has plenty of ideas of her own, so she both writes and illustrates her stories.

Pamela's idea for *Who Sank the Boat?* came about because she wanted to show what happens when you overload something. She hopes that everyone who reads this book will realise that it isn't the mouse's weight that causes the boat to sink, but the combined weight of everyone in that boat—the cow, the donkey, the sheep, the pig *and* the tiny little mouse.

Some authors remember something special from their childhood and they turn that into an idea for a story.

Peter Gouldthorpe loved going to Manly by ferry when he was a boy. He said it was always a very special outing and he imagined lots of things that could happen. So he sat down and put those memories into words and pictures, creating *Jonah and the Manly Ferry.*

First there was Frances
(My first ideas) Bob Graham

1.

Here is Frances on her horse. We know Frances very well. The strange thing is...

9.

You won't know that Frances used to ride a horse in the circus. But that is another story.

8.

The real problem was what to leave out.

2. ... that there were always so many interesting things happening at her house,

3. it's difficult to remember just where my first idea came from.

4. It may have been the day the guinea pigs escaped,

or it could have been...

5. ...when our dog Oscar chased Nosy the ferret through the kitchen.

6. There was never a dull moment,

7. and there were lots of ideas.

All of the stories, ideas and illustrations for Bob Graham's books come from watching people — children and adults. His idea for *First there was Frances* came from friends of his whose family just grew like Frances's does in the book. If you read the dedication you will see that the book is

For Fay, the only person I ever saw with a Shetland pony in her kitchen.

So authors and illustrators find their ideas all around them, they are observant and notice everything that is happening. They also remember things from the past. Anything at all can spark an idea for a story — even a load of firewood.

17

Does it take long to write a story?

Bertie and the Bear

Pamela Allen

The Tram
to
Bondi Beach

Elizabeth Hathorn
Illustrated by Julie Vivas

Every author works at a different speed. If the idea is a good one, and the author is happy with it, then the story will flow much faster than when the idea is not right, or the author has not solved all the problems. Sometimes a story is never finished because it didn't begin with a good idea.

A story for a picture book can have very few words, like Pamela Allen's *Bertie and the Bear*, which has just 200 words, or it can have more than 1000 words, like Elizabeth Hathorn's *The Tram to Bondi Beach*. A story for a picture book is much shorter than a story for a reading book. Sometimes these long books can have 40 000 words or more. This can take an author a year, maybe two or even three years to write.

Nan Hunt began writing *Whistle up the Chimney*, which has about 600 words, on 28 March 1979.

- She finished the first draft on 1 April 1979, then she re-wrote it.
- She finished the second draft on 11 April 1979, then she re-wrote it.
- She finished the third draft on 16 April 1979, and this was the version that she sent to her editor.

The first draft was called *Ghost Trains*. By the second draft Nan had changed the title to *Half a Door From a Bogey Louvre*, and this was the story which arrived on my desk at the end of April 1979. In fact, we didn't change the title to *Whistle up the Chimney* until December 1980, after the story was set in type and all the pictures were finished.

When an illustrator is writing his own story he also prepares roughs of his illustrations before he contacts the editor. He has to think not only about the words, but also about the pictures he wants to draw and paint.

Bob Graham's first roughs for *First there was Frances*, were sent to a publishing house in early 1982, however this book was not published until the end of 1985. The reason for the delay was that Bob hadn't fully worked out how to make his story, which has dozens of characters, flow naturally.

So Bob put this idea aside and went on and wrote and illustrated two other books, *Pearl's Place* and *Libby, Oscar and Me*, then he came back to *First there was Frances* and this time it worked.

If a story does not work for you after a lot of trying, it is a good idea to do what Bob Graham did and put it aside for a while. When you go back to it you will be surprised how easy it is to fix and write.

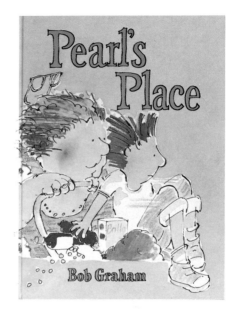

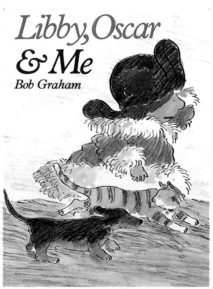

Finding the right illustrator

When the author and the editor are satisfied that the story is the best the author can make it, then the editor has to find the right illustrator.

For Nan Hunt's story *Whistle up the Chimney*, I needed an illustrator who liked the story, who could draw steam trains as well as people and who had an imagination and a sense of fun to appreciate and visualise Nan's marvellous words. I found the ideal illustrator in Craig Smith.

Finding the right illustrator is not always as easy as it sounds because the illustrator must like the author's story — it's no use trying to illustrate something you don't like because it shows in the work you do. The illustrator must have an understanding of the author's words. He must be able to bring those words to life, and to add all those little extras that belong with the story, even though the author may have forgotten to mention them.

If you look at a copy of *Whistle up the Chimney*, you will see a lovely, ginger tomcat on almost every page. However, when you read the text you find that Nan Hunt never mentions a cat. Craig added him in and gave him such a personality that Nan had to sit down and write a story for him — and that was how the second book, *An Eye Full of Soot*, was born. It tells of Tom Bola's adventures when he falls on to the express train and is whisked off into the night.

A *Pet for Mrs Arbuckle* was the first book Ann James illustrated. Ann needed to practise drawing all the wild animals in the book, and her own cat was the model for the gingernut cat.

Ann James drew the gingernut cat many times to get him just right.

We asked Ann to say where she got her ideas from.

Well, Mrs A is a bit like my mum, (she has a pair of bathers like Mrs A's, and the slippers were a present from my dad). The jumper she wears watering the garden is one my Gran knitted. The Gingernut cat was definitely my Ginger Cat called Cat who died last year at 14!

Two studies for Mrs Arbuckle.

Finding the right illustrator can take a long time, sometimes years, so the author has to learn to be very patient. Even when the editor has found an illustrator, it can take the illustrator months to think through his ideas and put them on paper. Quite often, even though he loves a story, an illustrator may not be able to put the right ideas on paper. Then the editor has to say 'no' and start looking for someone else.

Some stories present their illustrators with tremendous problems. When Julie Vivas was given Mem Fox's story *Possum Magic,* she had to work out how she could 'show' an 'invisible' character in her artwork. Look at a copy of this book and see how Julie managed to make Hush invisible, yet visible to the readers.

Junko Morimoto faced a similar problem in two of her books, *The Inch Boy* and *Mouse's Marriage.* In both of these books Junko's main character was very, very tiny. So that they wouldn't be lost or overlooked, she had to place them very carefully on each page. By doing this the characters became vivid and dynamic, and they catch the attention of the reader.

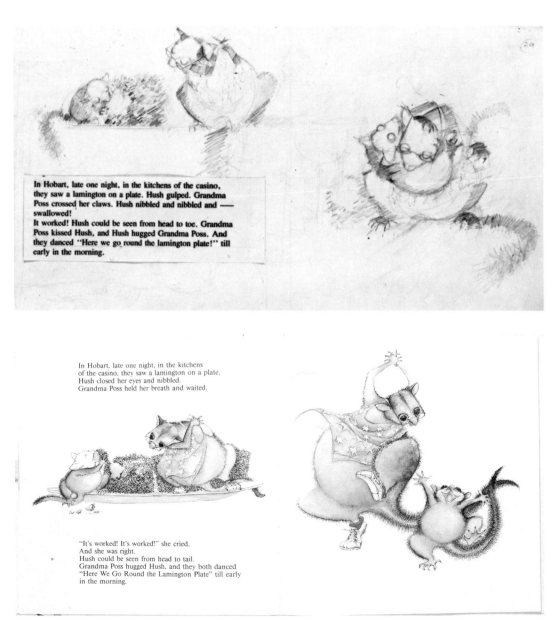

In Hobart, late one night, in the kitchens of the casino, they saw a lamington on a plate. Hush gulped. Grandma Poss crossed her claws. Hush nibbled and nibbled and —— swallowed!
It worked! Hush could be seen from head to toe. Grandma Poss kissed Hush, and Hush hugged Grandma Poss. And they danced "Here we go round the lamington plate!" till early in the morning.

In Hobart, late one night, in the kitchens of the casino, they saw a lamington on a plate. Hush closed her eyes and nibbled. Grandma Poss held her breath and waited.

"It's worked! It's worked!" she cried. And she was right. Hush could be seen from head to tail. Grandma Poss hugged Hush, and they both danced "Here We Go Round the Lamington Plate" till early in the morning.

Illustrators are usually asked to provide pencil roughs of their drawings before starting on the final illustrations. This allows the author or the editor to comment on the way the artist has interpreted the story and characters. In the case of this page from *Possum Magic* both the text and the picture were changed after the roughs were done.
How many changes can you find?

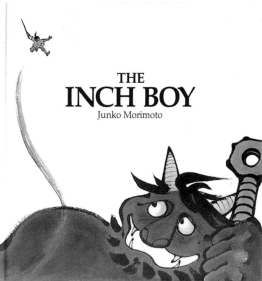

Sometimes, when a book is sold to a publisher in another country, the editor there will ask if she can change the text or the pictures. When *The Inch Boy* was sold to the United States the editor changed the cover design. Other changes might include words that are unfamiliar or spelt differently.

Doing it all again . . .

Many years ago, back in 1979, I went to stay with Nan Hunt at her home in Bathurst. One day we were driving past the show grounds and Nan pointed out a sign on one of the cottages—it read THE COTTAGE GATE. We both thought this had to be an idea for a book and sure enough, not long after I was back in my office in Sydney, a new story arrived from Nan, *Mary at the Cottage Gate*, all about a girl waiting for her aunt and uncle to take her to a country show.

Ever since then I have wanted to publish this story. I have given it to nine or ten different illustrators over the years, but not one of them has been able to capture the quality of the text.

At the end of 1984, I at long last found the right illustrator, Betina Ogden. She caught the spirit of a country show and, after a lot of rough drawings and editorial discussions, when several problems were sorted out (such as having the horses' legs going the right way for trotting), Betina was able to begin the final artwork.

This was delivered in November 1985. The designer now took over and checked everything, decided on the type he would use and had the story (now called *The Show*), typeset and ready for the printer.

Everything was carefully packed and dispatched to the printer in Hong Kong. And that's the last time we saw it. The parcel arrived safely at the printers, but over the Christmas holiday they had their offices cleaned and the cleaners threw out all the artwork!

The worst job in all my life was to telephone Betina and tell her that all her work had been destroyed. However, all is not lost, Betina has decided to do the book again, so it should be published before the end of this decade.

1. BEFORE CALL

2. DURING CALL

3. AFTER CALL

4. BEFORE NEXT CALL

5. NEXT CALL

. . . and again, and again

DEVELOPING DRAWINGS FOR "LIBBY, OSCAR & ME"

1st Sketch
Emily starts as a rather timid person

2nd Sketch
She then gets a dog...

3rd Sketch
... and starts to dress-up

4th Sketch
She becomes very out-going

5th Sketch
The previous ideas are combined to give her personality

Another picture book that was painted twice was *John Brown, Rose and the Midnight Cat.* The illustrator, Ron Brooks, planned the whole book, carefully drawing up each page and deciding where Jenny Wagner's text would fit within his artwork. Ron then sent all this to his editor who didn't like Ron's interpretation of the text, saying that it was not suitable. So Ron began again. This second version has become a firm favourite with everyone.

As you can see—it can take many years to make and publish a picture book.

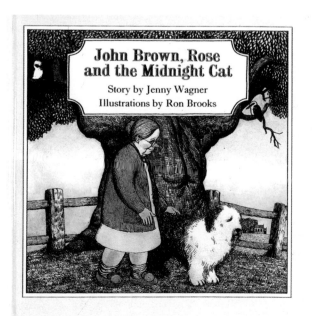

John Brown, Rose and the Midnight Cat

Story by Jenny Wagner
Illustrations by Ron Brooks

What size? What shape?

The story has been edited, the illustrator has been chosen and is ready to begin work, but what size is the book to be—and what shape?

These questions are usually resolved by the content of the story itself.

There are three basic shapes used for picture books:

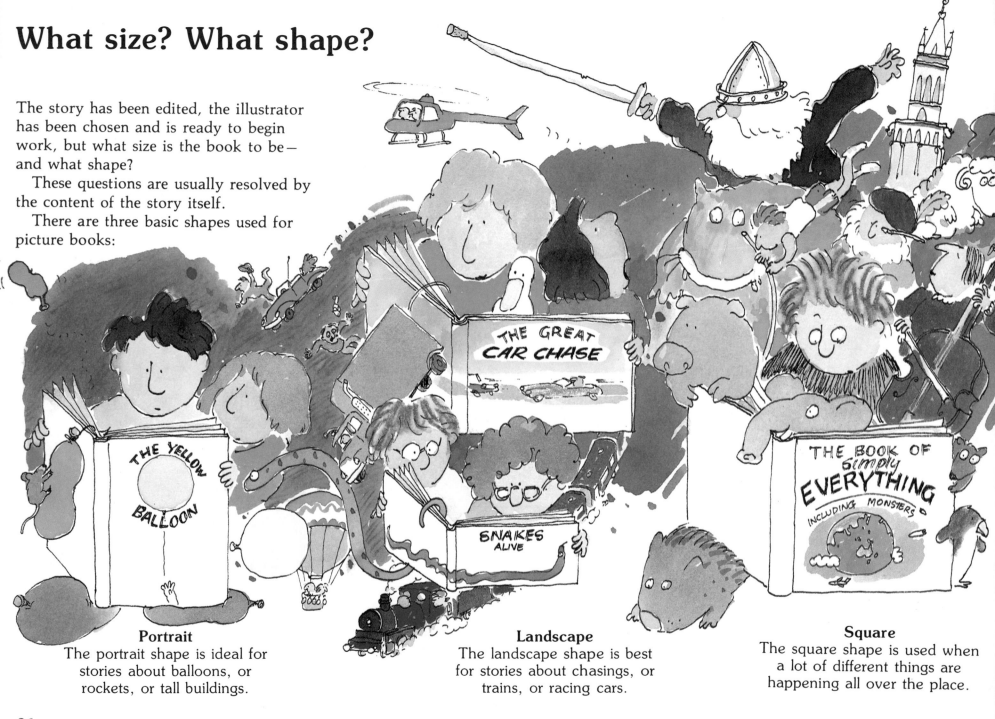

Portrait
The portrait shape is ideal for stories about balloons, or rockets, or tall buildings.

Landscape
The landscape shape is best for stories about chasings, or trains, or racing cars.

Square
The square shape is used when a lot of different things are happening all over the place.

26

Sometimes a book will change shape in an illustrator's mind. This is what happened with Bob Graham's book *First there was Frances*. Bob was both the author and the illustrator of this story.

When Bob first started planning his story and pictures, he thought about it as a portrait-shaped book. However, the story began to grow and Bob's ideas began to expand. This story is a cumulative one, which means more and more people and things are added each time the page is turned. Bob realised that to fit them all in he needed a landscape-shaped book.

The shape of a picture book is very important and it is one of the things that the illustrator always spends a lot of time thinking about. He also talks to the editor and designer to see what they think. The wrong shape can ruin the story.

The cover for *First there was Frances* was changed three times before Bob Graham and I were happy with it. The first version was a portrait shape which didn't suit the large number of characters that had to be fitted into each page. The second version was too quiet. The third version was just right except for one important detail: can you see what was changed in the final version?

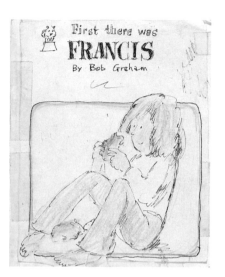

Version 1

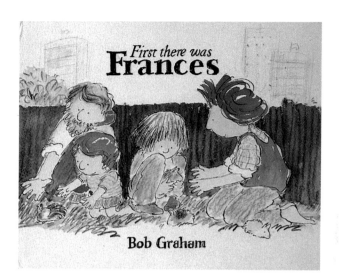

Version 2

Version 3

Version 4

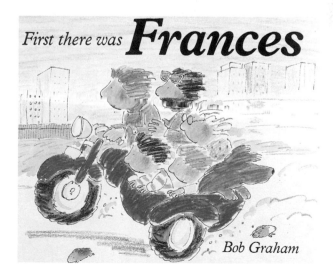

What medium?

Having chosen both the size and the shape for the book, the illustrator then has to decide what medium he will use for his illustrations. That is, whether he will use pen and ink, or a colour wash, or oils, or linocuts, or collage, or maybe a combination of the lot.

Again, it will be the content of the story that will help him make this decision.

Look at these books and see how the illustrator uses the different media to create specific effects:

In *Turramulli the Giant Quinkin* (above right) Percy Trezise and Dick Roughsey painted in acrylic, a thick and fast-drying medium.

In *The Useless Donkeys* (below right) Judith Cowell has used pieces of old lace for the curtain and dress material for the chair, as well as water colour. The illustrations took three years to complete.

Everyone shouted to make themselves heard. The baby was frightened and had to be cuddled, but the children were noisy, excited, as mad as the storm. They giggled and hooted, and raced round the house in the craziest games, leaping on tables, and bouncing on beds.
"The floods will be up by tomorrow," they told one another.

Mummy is on a diet.
She eats lettuce, tomato and cheese.
My big brother eats peanut butter sandwiches.
I eat honey sandwiches.
The hippopotamus on our roof eats cake all the time.

We're taking off ...
Whoopee – oh, wow!

For *Jonah and the Manly Ferry* Peter Gouldthorpe worked in linocuts. The three illustrations on the right show his experiments with colour. Each linocut has been printed in a different ink and then hand tinted. The picture below was the one accepted for the book.

Deborah Niland used ink and water colour in *There's a Hippopotamus on our Roof Eating Cake* (above left). Gwenda Turner's *Snow Play* is drawn in pencil with a colour wash added (below left).

Planning the book

Because it costs so much to print full colour picture books, you will find that nowadays they are usually only 32 pages in length—sometimes even as few as 24 pages are used. Each page is carefully planned. A picture book works like this:

When you have turned back the cover, the first double opening is the endpaper.

Turn the page and you will notice that the left-hand side of this next double opening is plain white. This is the back of your endpaper. If you look carefully you will see that about 5mm of this page is stuck into the right-hand page, making it hard to open it flat.

All this is to do with the binding of the book. The endpapers are a part of the binding. They can be used to make a book attractive, but their real job is to help in holding the book together—to give it strength so that it won't fall to pieces the first time it's opened.

The page opposite the back of the endpaper is page 1. This is usually called the half-title page and normally only the title of the book is printed here. Occasionally the illustrator will add a decoration.

Page 2 is the next left-hand page. This is often called the copyright page because it gives all the information as to who owns the story and the illustrations. This ownership is called copyright.

This page also gives all the information about the book—who did the typesetting and the printing, the name of the publisher and sometimes the editor's and designer's names.

It usually includes the dedication. Most authors like to 'give' their book to a special friend, so they put in a dedication.

Also on page 2 is the ISBN, which is short for International Standard Book Number. Every book printed in the world has its own special ISBN, which means it can be traced by anyone in any country. The ISBN number is also used by the bookseller and the publisher to simplify the ordering of stock, and by librarians for inter-library loans.

Then there is the CIP information—the cataloguing-in-publication data— which is supplied to the publisher by the National Library in Canberra and gives the Dewey decimal classification for each book. This makes it easier to find a book on a particular subject when you are at your library.

Page 3 is usually the title page. It gives you the title of the book, the author, the illustrator and the publisher. Sometimes the illustrator will add a painting here, sometimes it is left plain.

Turn the page to the first double opening—pages 4 and 5. This is where the story and illustrations begin. From here through to pages 30-31, there are fourteen double openings (or 28 pages) for the text and artwork.

Then there is one final page, a left-hand page, number 32. Here the illustrator can place the final piece of text, or just an illustration, or both.

The right-hand page of this opening is a plain page, because it is the back of the endpaper. The final double opening is the back endpaper which is usually the same as the front endpaper.

It is essential that the illustrator plans the whole book *before* he starts to paint. If he doesn't, he is likely to run out of pages halfway through, or finish too soon and have pages to spare.

When planning each opening the illustrator has a lot to think about. He must be certain that he is illustrating the words he wants on that page. He must also be aware of the important parts of the story and not have half the text on one page and half on the next and so upset the flow of the story.

There is no need for the illustrator to put the text on one page and his artwork on the other, although it sometimes works best this way. The whole book must be thought through and planned, not only by the illustrator but also by the editor and the designer—it is a team effort.

Sometimes an illustrator will make a little "map" of the pages like this. He or she can then decide on the number of words per page before they start the pictures.

Final page

And Morris sadly slopped into the boggy slush.

32.
28.

Back of endpaper (stuck to 5mm of page 32)

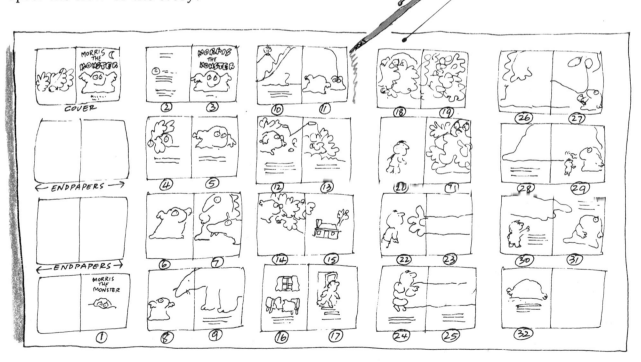

Choosing the typeface

The author types her final manuscript on a typewriter, or a word processor, and sends this to her editor. The alphabet letters, or characters, made by these machines are not suitable to use in a picture book, for many reasons — they are too small, they are hard to read, they are not spaced correctly, or they don't look right with the illustrations. This is the reason why all stories have to be typeset.

Type comes in different faces (at right). Type sizes are measured in points (below).

6 pt

12 pt

24 pt

36 pt

48 pt

Typography is the word used for the skill of choosing the right typeface that works with both the story and the illustrations. It is a very important part of the designer's job.

There are hundreds of different typefaces for the designer to choose from — and dozens of different sizes. Here are some of the typefaces you are likely to find in the books you read:

Helvetica	Once upon a time
Plantin	Once upon a time
Souvenir	Once upon a time
Avant Garde	Once upon a time
Schoolbook	Once upon a time
Times	Once upon a time
Garamond	Once upon a time
Baskerville	Once upon a time

So the designer has two things to consider when he is choosing the type for a book — the typeface and the type size.

For the book you are holding the designer has chosen Paladium typeface, which he has had set in 12pt size. His reasons were that it had to be clear and easy to read, and it also had to work with the various styles of artwork and photographs used in the book.

So that the words of the story can be printed at the same time as the illustrations, they are typeset on to a special paper, which is similar to the paper used for photographs. It is called a bromide, or a repro. This process is called

1. The author types her final manuscript and,

2. sends it to her editor.

either phototypesetting or photocomposition, and it is done with:

- a keyboard—where the story is typed in
- a computer— where it is all stored
- a typesetter—which makes the type on the repro.

A photocopy of the repro, called a galley, is always sent to the editor for her to check that the spelling and punctuation are correct. Sometimes the person at the keyboard hits the wrong key, so everything must be checked and double checked.

Once the editor, author and designer are all certain that everything is correct, then the repro of the story is ready for the next process—this is the printing of the book.

3. The editor makes a final check and gives it to,

4. the designer who chooses the type

The designer gives instructions to the typesetter

MORRIS
THE MONSTER

1. Set text in 14pt Paladium.
2. Set line for line.

5. The typesetter sets all the type on a Keyboard. It is held on a computer.

6. The words are processed onto long strips of photographic paper.

7. The editor, author and designer check the repro. for mistakes.

This is called bromide or repro.

8. Off to the printer.

The right paper

Chipper

Refiner

Dandy R

Pulp
Digester

Bleacher

Cleaners

Debarker
(nothing to do
with noisy dogs)

Washer

Every book needs paper, but not all the papers are the same — some are thick, some are thin, some have a shiny surface, others a dull surface. Each one is different and each behaves in a different way when the inks are printed on its surface.

The designer and the editor must choose a paper that will react in the right way when the particular style of artwork is printed on it.

Most papers nowadays are made from wood, straw or a special grass (called esparto). Paper is made by turning the wood into a pulp — just like a gooey porridge — which is floated in water and fed into a paper-making machine. Slowly all the water is squeezed out leaving only the fibres behind. These fibres are caught together and form what looks like a giant spider web.

Occasionally paper is made from other materials like cotton, linen or the ends of rope, but mostly wood is used. It can be made from a mixture of all these materials, or from one only.

Paper is delivered to the printer in huge rolls or flat sheets ready to fit on to the printing machines.

The paper used for newspapers or magazines is not meant to last a long time, so a cheap paper is used which sometimes looks very grey and dirty and tears easily.

For a picture book, the type of paper that is used is very important. If the paper is cheap the grey colour will change all the illustrations, and if it is too thin, the illustrations from one page show through to the next page, which make the

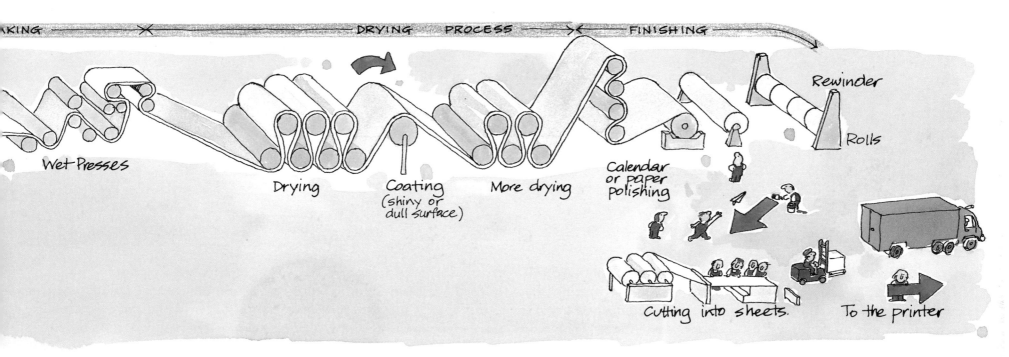

Rewinder

Rolls

Wet Presses

Drying

Coating
(shiny or
dull surface)

More drying

Calendar
or paper
Polishing

Cutting into sheets.

To the printer

book look confused and messy.

In the book you are holding we used 120 gsm matt art paper. This is a bright, white paper, and it is strong, which is important in a picture book which is read and handled frequently.

Because all papers are very thin, it is easier to measure it by its weight, rather than by its thickness. The weight of 120 gsm used in this book means that it is '120 grams per square metre'. The matt art, which was chosen, is a paper which is of a high quality but not shiny. We chose this because the type of artwork used by Bob Graham looks best when it is reproduced on this kind of paper.

For the endpapers, which need a heavier paper because they help to strengthen the binding, the weight used was 140 gsm.

The illustration which is on the cover of this book was printed and then laminated. Lamination is a very thin coating of clear plastic which is applied to the surface and which gives it a shiny or gloss finish.

The printed and laminated sheet was then pasted on to a 6000 ums (three millimetres) board. This board is really a cardboard. Hard cover books, such as this one, are referred to as having 'laminated papercovered boards' for their covers.

With paperbacks, the cover illustration will be printed on a much heavier paper than is used inside the book. This is because the cover has to protect the book. Again, the cover will often be laminated for extra protection.

Colour separation

Craig Smith's artwork is ready for separation at the printer's (at left).

On the right is an enlargement of a small part of the picture on the left. In it you can see that Mrs Mack's face and her cat are made up of hundreds of tiny dots.

Runaway dot

Finally, after months, sometimes years, of work, everything is ready to send to the printer.

The original artwork painted by the illustrator cannot be used, as it is, by the printer on his machines. The artwork has to be turned into a film before it can be printed, just as the author's words were typeset and turned into a bromide, or repro.

A person, called a colour separator, is responsible for taking the illustrator's paintings and making them into a film. This is done by attaching each piece of artwork to a cylinder, which means that the illustrator should always do his paintings on a lightweight board that will bend around this cylinder. If the paintings

are done on a thick cardboard, they have to be carefully sliced off, like cheese, and later glued back together.

Once the artwork has been carefully attached to the cylinder, the colour separator turns on his special camera. This camera moves around the cylinder taking four separate photographs of each piece of artwork.

The first photograph that is taken shows only the yellow areas of the artwork, the second the red areas, the third the blue and the fourth the black. This process is called colour-scanning, because it scans or takes out each colour.

The four sheets of film, for each piece of artwork, are referred to as the colour separations. The image on each film is

made up of a pattern of dots. This film does not have any actual colour on it, only the patterns of the dots which indicate where the yellow, red, blue or black will be printed, and in what strength.

If you look at a full colour illustration in a picture book through a magnifying glass, you will see that it is made up of dots. The dots of each colour are of different sizes but they lie close together, or on top of each other, so that when you look at a picture book with your naked eye all the colours are blended as the illustrator intended.

The separation process: the original illustration (at left) is separated into four colours (below). The colours are mixed by printing each colour on top of the previous one.

Yellow

Magenta

Cyan

Black

Magenta is printed over the yellow.

Then cyan is added.

Finally black completes the picture.

Ready to print

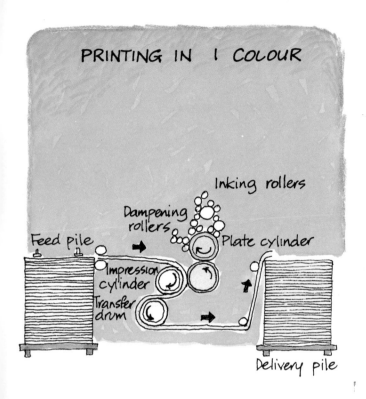

PRINTING IN 1 COLOUR

Inking rollers

Dampening rollers

Feed pile

Plate cylinder

Impression cylinder

Transfer drum

Delivery pile

PRINTING IN 4 COLOURS

The printer now has to transfer each one of those four colour separations on to four metal plates (the process is called plate making), ready for printing. Each plate is wrapped around a press cylinder on his printing machine. This cylinder is then inked with the colour that is stated on the original colour separation. The colours are printed one at a time. The colour sequence varies from printer to printer. In the above illustration, yellow is

first, then red, blue, and finally the black plate, which also includes the words of the story.

When each of these four colour plates hits a rubber blanket, that in turn hits a piece of paper, then, amazingly, we have a reproduction of the original illustration being printed.

However, they don't always come out exactly right the first time. This is why the designer always asks the printer to

send him colour proofs of each illustration. These proofs are then checked and the printer makes adjustments to his printing machine, until everything is as near as possible to the original illustration.

Sometimes the printer seems to have problems with one particular colour. When this happens the designer will ask to see two, three or even four lots of colour proofs. Some of the bright,

iridescent colours used by Dick Roughsey and Percy Trezise in their Aboriginal legend, *The Quinkins*, were very difficult to reproduce. In these cases the printer will often use a special ink to help capture the effects of the original artwork.

All the way through this book we have been calling everything a full colour picture book. This point is not correct. As you have just seen, these so-called 'full colour' books are actually made up of just three colours—plus black, which adds the details and which is used to print the text.

A skilled printer can actually make up unlimited different hues (colours) just by mixing those three inks in various dot strengths, sometimes using only two of the colours, other times all three. However, if you want a real black then black ink must be added because the other three together are just not strong enough.

The printer's inks used are not the same colours that you will find in your paint box. The yellow is a pure, bright yellow; the blue (usually called cyan) is a cold, bright blue; while the red (called magenta) is a pinkish red. These inks are not clear and runny, like drawing inks, but are thick and gooey and almost solid. However, they are translucent when printed.

Printing and binding

Books are not printed one page at a time. Usually eight, sixteen or even thirty-two pages are printed at once on one side of the sheet, while on the other side the same number is being done. (This is called a 'back-up' sheet.)

The above illustration shows how most picture books are printed, 'eight pages to view', 'back-up', then folded, trimmed and gathered ready for binding into their case.

This set of sixteen folded sheets, which are pages 9 to 24, will be slipped inside

another set of sixteen folded pages, these will be page numbers 1 to 8 and 25 to 32. Now a thirty-two page picture book is ready for sewing, trimming and binding.

The folded sheets are sewn together, with a double thread for extra strength, and this is also all done by a machine. The reason for the sewing is to hold all the pages together, in the right order, before they are glued and put into their covers—or 'cased-in' as it is called.

However, before they go to the machine

for the gluing and casing-in, all the untidy edges have to be trimmed off the pages. A machine, called a guillotine or three-knife trimmer, is used for this and it cuts all three edges at the one time. Great care must be taken by the person operating this machine or the books end up with very crooked pages. About 2000-3000 books can be trimmed in an hour.

The next process, the casing-in, is also done by machine and is a fully automatic one. The printed insides of the book are

Casing-in and applying paste to endpapers

Trimming on three sides

Two sections sewn together through the spine

Gluing

now firmly glued inside their covers. The endpapers are stuck in during this process.

The book you are holding has two-colour endpapers. They have been glued to the inside of the covers and then slightly glued to pages 1 and 48. You will notice when you open this book that the first and last papers don't open out flat. Never force them to open, they are not meant to, they are there to help hold the inside of the book in its covers.

The illustration for the cover of the book is treated separately. It is printed separately, then it has to be specially glued to the boards that are going to make up the covers of the book. It also has the glossy lamination added over it for protection.

Paperback books are printed in the same way as hardcover books. But their bindings can be different. Sometimes, instead of sewing the sheets together, they are glued. This is a cheaper process and helps keep the cost of the paperback down.

A paperback book has a 'drawn on cover'. This means that the cover has been creased to fit round the spine of the book, then glued on to the inside of the spine (it is also glued a little way on to the inside of the front and back covers). It is then placed round the text and the whole lot is cut, or guillotined, at the one time on the same machine. This method saves both time and money.

From the printer to you

The picture book is finally printed, all the copies are packed carefully into cartons (if they are badly packed the books will be damaged), and they are ready to leave the printer.

The printer always sends about one hundred advance, or early, copies of the book to the editor so that she can make certain that the author and illustrator receive a copy. She also has to be sure that every salesperson has a copy and that they know all about the book and how special it is. The editor also talks to the publicity people about it so that they can arrange for interviews and reviews with newspapers, radio and television.

From the printer the books go to the publisher's warehouse. This is a huge building, usually in the suburbs or even in a country town, where the publisher keeps the stock of all books that he wants to sell to the bookseller.

The books are stored in the warehouse for a couple of months before they reach the bookshops. This is because the salespeople have to visit all the booksellers and collect their orders—and the orders have to be picked out of the warehouse, charged (or invoiced) to the bookseller and delivered to her.

Because Australia is such a large country, each salesperson is given a certain territory to look after. If they are in the city they can visit each bookshop once a week. However, if their territory is all in the north of Queensland it takes much longer.

Each salesperson carries a large suitcase of new books to show to the bookseller, so the editor likes to make certain that the books she has helped create are also favourites with the salespeople. To do this she must talk to them as much as possible and send them information about the authors and illustrators.

The salespeople collect their orders together and send them to the warehouse. Here the books are picked off the shelves, invoiced and packed, before being sent to the bookseller.

Finally the books reach the bookshop. The bookseller unpacks them, checking that the invoice is correct and that she had been sent the books she ordered. She then puts the new books out on display—if the author is lucky she may put up a special display in her shop, or even in her window.

Now the picture book, that has taken so long to make, is ready to be purchased by your parents, your teachers, your librarians, or by you . . .

Next time you open a brand new book just remember how many people worked together as a team to make it . . . and remember too, how many years it took to reach you. But most important of all, *enjoy reading it.*

Making a picture book

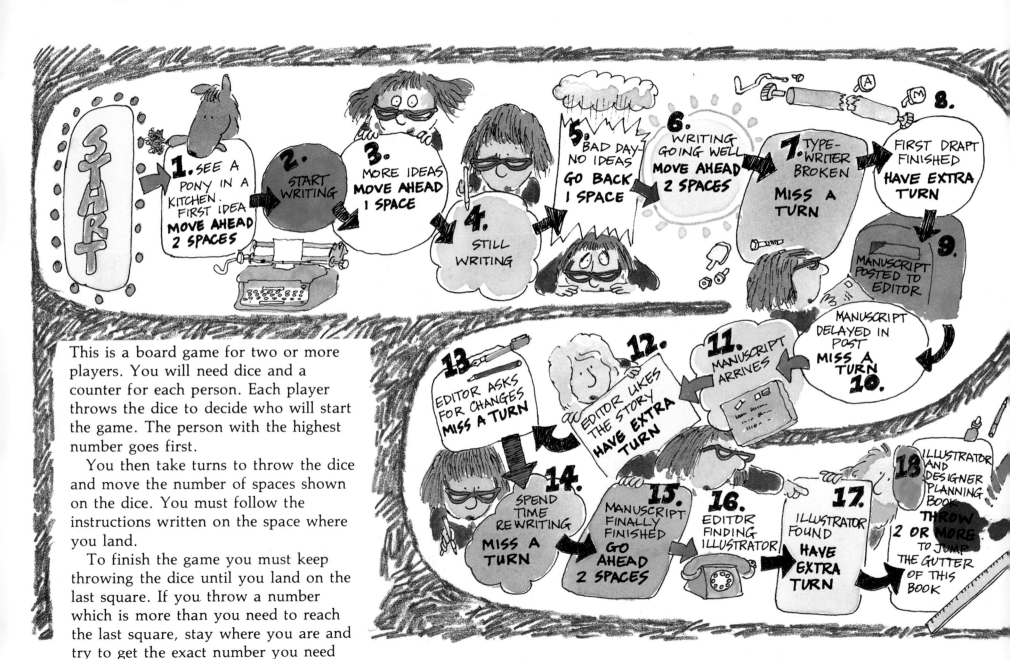

This is a board game for two or more players. You will need dice and a counter for each person. Each player throws the dice to decide who will start the game. The person with the highest number goes first.

You then take turns to throw the dice and move the number of spaces shown on the dice. You must follow the instructions written on the space where you land.

To finish the game you must keep throwing the dice until you land on the last square. If you throw a number which is more than you need to reach the last square, stay where you are and try to get the exact number you need on your next turn.

Publisher's pursuit

All these questions can be answered after reading this book. Try them out with a friend.

[1] How many times did Mem Fox rewrite *Possum Magic?*
[Page 13]

[2] Whose fire made the sound 'biddly-dum biddly-dee'?
[Page 14]

[3] Name three Australian picture books with ginger cats in them.
[Pages 20-21]

[4] Which Australian children's book artist was told her paintings had just been thrown out in the rubbish?
[Page 24]

[5] Judith Cowell used three different media to illustrate *The Useless Donkeys.* Can you name them?
[Page 28]

[6] What well-known picture book was first called *Hush the Invisible Mouse?*
[Page 13]

[7] What do the letters ISBN stand for?
[Page 30]

[8] How many colours are normally used to print a full colour picture book?
[Pages 37]

[9] Name a picture book that was painted by two artists.
[Pages 28, 39]

[10] What household object has a spine and a case and is made from sheets?
[Pages 40-41]

Bibliography

BERTIE AND THE BEAR written and illustrated by Pamela Allen (Nelson)

AN EYE FULL OF SOOT by Nan Hunt, illustrated by Craig Smith (Collins)

FIRST THERE WAS FRANCES written and illustrated by Bob Graham (Lothian)

THE INCH BOY adapted by Helen Smith, illustrated by Junko Morimoto (Collins)

JOHN BROWN, ROSE AND THE MIDNIGHT CAT by Jenny Wagner, illustrated by Ron Brooks (Viking Kestrel)

JONAH AND THE MANLY FERRY written and illustrated by Peter Gouldthorpe (Methuen)

LIBBY, OSCAR AND ME written and illustrated by Bob Graham (Lothian)

MOUSE'S MARRIAGE adapted by Anne Bower Ingram, illustrated by Junko Morimoto (Lothian)

PEARL'S PLACE written and illustrated by Bob Graham (Lothian)

A PET FOR MRS ARBUCKLE by Gwenda Smyth, illustrated by Ann James (Nelson)

POSSUM MAGIC by Mem Fox, illustrated by Julie Vivas (Omnibus Books)

THE QUINKINS by Percy Trezise and Dick Roughsey (Collins)

SNOW PLAY written and illustrated by Gwenda Turner (Collins)

THERE'S A HIPPOPOTAMUS ON OUR ROOF EATING CAKE by Hazel Edwards, illustrated by Deborah Niland (Hodder & Stoughton)

THE TRAM TO BONDI BEACH by Elizabeth Hathorn, illustrated by Julie Vivas (Methuen)

TURRAMULLI THE GIANT QUINKIN by Percy Trezise and Dick Roughsey (Collins)

THE USELESS DONKEYS by Lydia Pender, illustrated by Judith Cowell (Methuen)

WHISTLE UP THE CHIMNEY by Nan Hunt, illustrated by Craig Smith (Collins)

WHO SANK THE BOAT? written and illustrated by Pamela Allen (Nelson)

Acknowledgements

The author and publisher wish to thank the following people and publishers for permission to reproduce artwork and other material in this book: Peter Gouldthorpe, p. 29; Nan Hunt, p. 15; Ann James, p. 21; Julie Vivas, pp. 13, 22; Collins: *An Eye Full of Soot*, p. 20; *The Inch Boy*, p. 23; *Snow Play*, p. 29; *Turramulli the Giant Quinkin*, p. 28; *Whistle up the Chimney*, pp. 14, 15, 20, 36; Hodder & Stoughton: *There's a Hippopotamus on our Roof Eating Cake*, p. 29; Lothian: *First there was Frances*, p. 27; *Libby, Oscar and Me*, p. 19; *Pearl's Place*, p. 19; Nelson: *A Pet for Mrs Arbuckle*, pp. 20, 21; *Bertie and the Bear*, p. 18; *Who Sank the Boat?* p. 16; Omnibus: *Possum Magic*, pp. 13, 22; Viking Kestrel: *John Brown, Rose and the Midnight Cat*, p. 25.

Every effort has been made to trace the holder of copyright of the illustrative material contained in this book. Where the attempt has been unsuccessful the publisher would be pleased to hear from the artist/publisher to rectify any omission.

Answers to publisher's pursuit

1 Twenty-five.
2 Mrs Millie Mack in *Whistle up the Chimney*.
3 *A Pet for Mrs Arbuckle, Whistle up the Chimney, An Eye Full of Soot*. There are others.
4 Betina Ogden.
5 Watercolour, bits of old lace, bits of dress material.
6 *Possum Magic*.
7 International Standard Book Number.
8 Four (yellow, magenta, cyan and black).
9 *The Quinkins* or *Turramulli the Giant Quinkin*. There are others.
10 A hardcover picture book.

Index

Text – 1st Draft – 26.2.86

Returned to ABI – 4.3.86

ABI returned to Methuen – 27.3.86

Making a Picture Book

by

Anne Bower Ingram

METHUEN
Sydney

Anne's first draft

THE BEGINNINGS OF THE BOOK

— prefer my original text will accept

thousands of years (people) — NOT people ...it may

For ~~centuries man~~ had scratched picture-symbols on bone
or stone, on the walls of caves or pyramids, when ~~he they~~ wanted to record the stories of ~~their~~ ~~his~~ people or the number
of animals ~~he~~ had exchanged for corn.

Next, a kind of paper, papyrus, was used by the Egyptians,
Greeks and Romans. This was made by crushing the pitch
found in the stems of the papyrus plant. Later still a
material called vellum, or parchment, was made from the
skins of animals.

p. ?

The first real paper seems to have been invented in China
and ~~this had~~ reached Europe about the 8th century via
Arabia. The first books, called manuscripts, appeared in
Europe during the 9th century. These were all handwritten
and painted, usually by monks living in monasteries, it
~~therefore~~ took years just to make one book.

Not used

It was the invention of moving type and printing that
changed all this and made books available to everyone.
This invention has been credited to Johann GUTENBERG, a
German living during the 15th century.

No longer was each book slowly written by hand, now it
was possible to print lots of copies of the same book,
quickly and cheaply. This made books available to everyone
who could read.

Anne. We think maybe this page doesn't belong in the book. Page 3 unless a brighter opening & more to the point.

(illustrated time line)

(Blocks of text above could be arranged along the time line)

Could be made subject of a boxed para.:
If it took six days to write and illustrate one page of the bible, how long would it take to ...... an?